New Curriculum

Primary
Science

Learn, practise and revise

Year 4

Alan Jarvis and
William Merrick

RISING★STARS

Rising Stars UK Ltd, 7 Hatchers Mews, Bermondsey Street, London SE1 3GS

www.risingstars-uk.com

All facts are correct at the time of going to press.

Published 2013

Authors: Alan Jarvis and William Merrick

Text design: Green Desert Ltd

Cover design: West 8 Design

Illustrations: Oxford Designers and Illustrators; David Woodroffe

Publisher: Camilla Erskine

Editorial: Sparks (www.sparkspublishing.com)

British Library Cataloguing in Publication Data.

A CIP record for this book is available from the British Library.

ISBN: 978-0-85769-683-0

Printed by Craft Print International Ltd, Singapore

Contents

How to get the best out of this book

Each topic spreads across two pages and focuses on one major idea. Many of your lessons may be based on these topics. Each double page helps you to keep **On track** and **Aiming higher**.

Title and key ideas: tell you what you are aiming to learn. The second idea is always more difficult than the first.

Key information: sets out the key facts that you need to know and the ideas you need to understand fully.

Key questions: help you to learn more facts and understand the science in each topic. The investigations you do will give you the evidence you need to prove the scientific facts you've learnt.

Key words and their meanings: help build up your scientific vocabulary. Remember that some words mean one thing in everyday life and something more special in science.

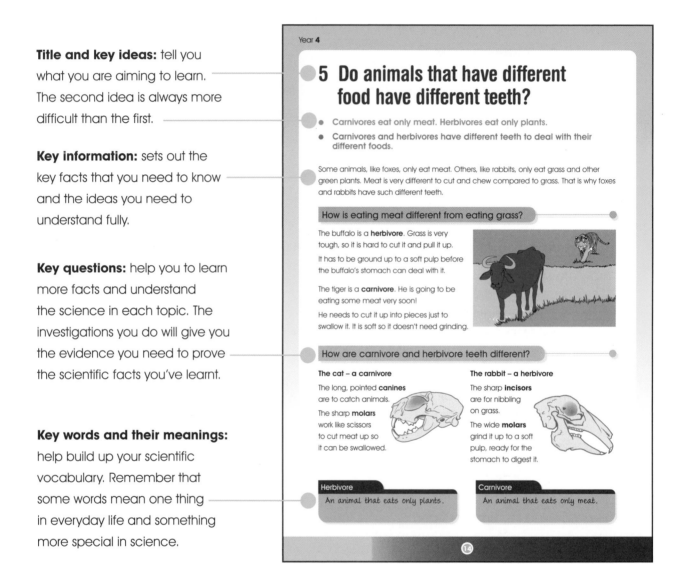

Follow these simple rules if you are using the book for revising.

1 Read each page carefully. Give yourself time to take in each idea.

2 Learn the key facts and ideas. Ask your teacher or mum, dad or the adult who looks after you if you need help.

3 Concentrate on the things you find more difficult.

4 Only work for about 20 minutes or so at a time. Take a break and then do more work.

The right-hand page has lots of fun questions for you to try. They help you to find how well you have understood what you have learned. There are questions on facts, ideas and scientific investigations. If you are stuck, the information on the left-hand page will help.

If you get most of the **On track** questions right then you are working at the expected level for the year. Well done – that's brilliant! If you get most of the **Aiming higher** questions right, you are working at the top of expectations for your year. You're doing really well!

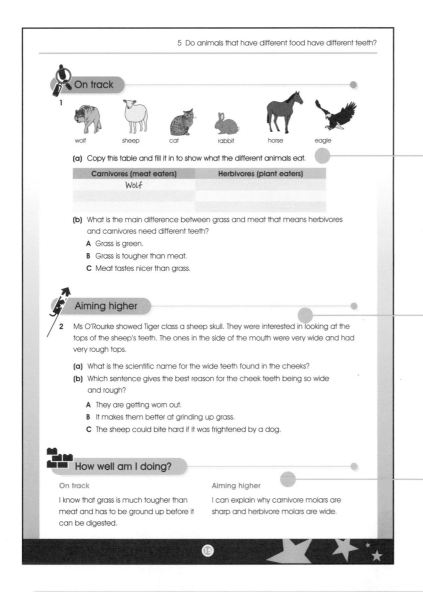

On track questions: come in different styles. Be sure to read each one carefully. Think about what the diagrams are telling you. Write your answers in your notebook.

Aiming higher questions: are more difficult. To answer them well, you have to know more facts or understand a harder idea. Write your answers in your notebook.

How well am I doing?: helps you to track progress. Keep a running record of how well you are doing so you keep on target.

Follow these simple rules if you want to know how well you are doing.

1 Work through the questions.

2 Check your answers with your teacher or using the answer booklet in the middle of the book.

3 Keep a record of how well you do.

4 Write down anything you are finding difficult and work through the chapter again to see if you can find the answer. If you are still finding it hard, ask your teacher for help.

1 What teeth have you got?

- Humans and animals have various types of teeth.
- The different types of teeth do different jobs.

Have you noticed that you bite an apple with your front teeth, but then you chew it with your back teeth? You have different teeth for different jobs. Let's see if they look different from each other.

What kinds of teeth do you have?

You can look at your own teeth in a mirror and feel them with your tongue.

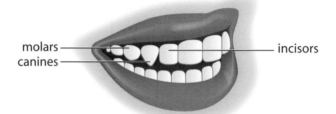

molars — incisors
canines —

The **incisors** are the front four teeth on the top, and also on the bottom. They are flat and sharp like chisels.

Next come the **canines.** They are the "fangs" in animals that bite! They are long and pointed.

The **molars** are the back teeth, sometimes called the cheek teeth. They are flat and wide.

What are the different teeth for?

Your sharp front teeth work like scissors to cut off pieces of food.

You can use your pointy canines to tear off tough pieces of meat.

Your flat molars grind up the food so you can swallow it.

Grind
To mash something up.

Swallow
To send something down from your mouth to the stomach.

On track

This is a drawing of the teeth normally found in Year 3 children.
There are 20 of them. They are called the first teeth, or **milk teeth**.

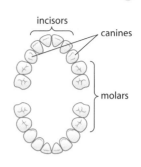

1   Count your own teeth. You can look in your mouth with a mirror,
    and also feel them with your tongue.

   (a) See if you can fill in this chart with the numbers of teeth
        you have.

My teeth	Top row	Bottom row
Incisors		
Canines		
Molars		
Total		

   (b) How many teeth have you got altogether?

   (c) How many of your new teeth have come through so far?

Aiming higher

2   Lucy looked at the teeth in her mouth.

   (a) These are the main jobs of your teeth.
        Match up each type of tooth to its job.

   A – grinding food up by chewing

   B – biting off pieces of things like apples.

   C – gripping and tearing tough food

   (b) Explain how the shape of an incisor tooth
        helps it to do its job.

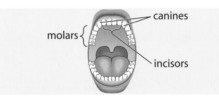

Name of tooth	Main job of tooth – A, B or C
incisor	
canine	
molar	

How well am I doing?

On track

I can describe the different kind of teeth
we have.

Aiming higher

I can explain how the shapes of the
different teeth help them do their special
jobs.

2 How can you look after your teeth?

- Humans only get two sets of teeth, so we need to look after them.
- There are many good ways of looking after our teeth and gums.

Have you lost any of your first teeth? Children in Year 4 usually have a few gaps. All of your first teeth will fall out one by one. A second set will replace them. Look after them – they have to last for the rest of your life!

Why do we lose our milk teeth?

Your first set of 20 teeth are called **milk teeth**.

They are just right for your small mouth. When you grow up, you will need bigger teeth. You will also have more – there will be 32.

It isn't a problem when a child loses a milk tooth. New ones soon grow. If a grown-up loses a tooth, it's a big shame. The gap will be there forever!

How can we look after our teeth?

Teeth can go bad and can give you toothache. This is called tooth decay and is caused by germs (**plaque bacteria**) growing on them. Sometimes a bad tooth has to be taken out. Brushing your teeth cleans the germs off.

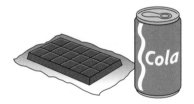

Sweets and sugary drinks will feed the germs that can rot teeth.

Carrots and apples are good as they have less sugar to feed the germs.

Brushing your teeth before you go to bed cleans the sugar and germs off.

Milk teeth
Your first set of teeth.

Decay
What happens when something rots.

On track

1   Katrina is seven years old. One of her front teeth has fallen out! Her mum says not to worry, as one will soon grow to take its place.

(a) What is the name given to your first set of teeth?

(b) How many sets of teeth will Katrina have altogether?

(c) Why do you need to replace your first teeth?

Aiming higher

2   Ms O'Rourke has made a list of good ideas to help Tiger class look after their teeth. Her first idea was:

> Brush your teeth twice a day.

(a) Write down two more rules she can put on her list.

(b) Explain why brushing your teeth makes them last longer.

How well am I doing?

On track

I can say how many sets of teeth I will have in my life.

Aiming higher

I can explain how to look after my teeth.

3 What is your digestive system?

- **The digestive system is the food tube that runs through our bodies.**
- **It breaks down and dissolves food so the rest of the body can use it.**

Eating food lets us grow bigger and stronger, because our bodies are made from the food we have eaten. Food also gives us the energy we need to keep warm and move. Food has to change a lot inside us before that can happen!

What is your digestive system?

The **digestive system** is a very long tube which goes all of the way from your mouth to your bottom. It is coiled up so it can fit neatly inside you.

These are its parts:

- **Mouth:** Tongue and teeth. The mouth chews the food to make it easy to swallow.
- **Oesophagus:** the tube that takes the food down to your stomach.
- **Stomach:** a bag that holds the food to start with. Some digestion happens here.
- **Intestines:** The coiled tubes that go the rest of the way through. Digestion is completed in there.

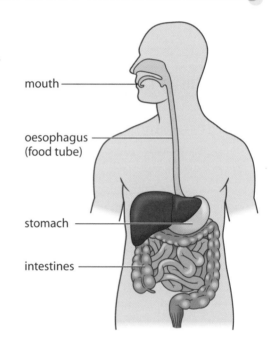

mouth

oesophagus (food tube)

stomach

intestines

What is digestion?

- Inside us, our food is turned into a soupy liquid. It is broken down and dissolved.
- Liquids called digestive juices in the mouth, stomach and intestines break down the food.
- Then the blood can absorb the dissolved food and carry it to wherever it is needed in the body.

Digestion	Absorb
The way food is broken down and dissolved ready for use.	To soak up.

On track

1 Copy out the table and match up these parts of the body to the descriptions.
The first one has been done for you.

mouth	oesophagus	tongue	stomach	teeth	intestine

	Description	Body part
(a)	Where the teeth and tongue are found	mouth
(b)	Grind up the food until it is soft for swallowing	
(c)	A long tube connecting the stomach to the bottom	
(d)	Takes food from the mouth to the stomach	
(e)	Helps us swallow our food, and also to taste it.	
(f)	A bag that holds the food. Some digestion happens here.	

Aiming higher

2 Copy out the flow chart and put these sentences in the correct boxes. The last
one has been done for you.

The chewed food and drink is all mixed up.
Dissolved food is carried away by the blood.
Chewing makes food smooth and soft.
Anything not needed passes out to the toilet.
More digestive juices finish dissolving the food.
Swallowed food is passed along to the stomach.

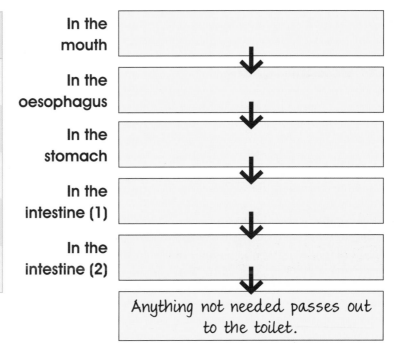

In the mouth

In the oesophagus

In the stomach

In the intestine (1)

In the intestine (2)

Anything not needed passes out to the toilet.

How well am I doing?

On track

I can name the different parts of the digestive system.

Aiming higher

I can explain how the digestive system breaks down and dissolves food.

4 What are food chains?

- Animals eat plants or other animals, but green plants can make their own food.
- You can show what animals eat by making a food chain.

Have you ever wondered where all the food in the world comes from? You might have chicken for dinner. What did the chicken eat? The farmer fed the chicken with grain such as corn. Where did the corn come from? That grew in a field. You can always track everything you eat back to a green plant growing in the first place.

What are predators, prey and producers?

The fox is a **predator**. That means he is a hunter. He eats rabbits.

The fox eats rabbits, so rabbits are the fox's **prey**. Rabbits eat green plants.

The green plants make the food to start with, so they are called the **producers.**

What is a food chain?

You can show your knowledge about what animals eat in a **food chain**.

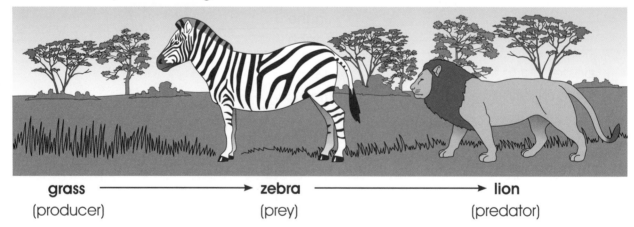

grass	→	zebra	→	lion
(producer)		(prey)		(predator)

The grass makes the food in the first place. Then the zebra eats the grass, and finally the lion eats the zebra. The food is being passed along the chain.

Producer
"Produce" means "make". Green plants produce the food that starts every food chain.

Consumer
"Consume" means "eat". Zebras and lions are both consumers.

On track

1 These animals like to eat different things.

cat

wheat

wolf

mouse

sheep

grass

Copy this table and put the names of the animals and plants into the correct columns, to show whether they are predator, prey or producers.

Predator	Prey	Producer

Aiming higher

2 Here are a few facts about some animals and what they eat.

Owls eat smaller birds

A caterpillar eats lettuce leaves

A thrush eats caterpillars

(a) Copy this table and show the information as a food chain.

(b) Look at the food chain you have made and name the following things:

- The producer
- Two predators
- Two prey animals

(c) Look again at question 1. Make two food chains using those animals and plants.

How well am I doing?

On track

I can say that predators eat other animals, which are called their prey.

Aiming higher

I can show what animals eat by making a food chain.

5 Do animals that eat different food have different teeth?

- Carnivores eat only meat. Herbivores eat only plants.
- Carnivores and herbivores have different teeth to deal with their different foods.

Some animals, like foxes, only eat meat. Others, like rabbits, only eat grass and other green plants. Meat is very different to cut and chew compared to grass. That is why foxes and rabbits have such different teeth.

How is eating meat different from eating grass?

The buffalo is a **herbivore**. Grass is very tough, so it is hard to cut it and pull it up.

It has to be ground up to a soft pulp before the buffalo's stomach can deal with it.

The tiger is a **carnivore**. He is going to be eating some meat very soon!

He needs to cut it up into pieces just to swallow it. It is soft so it doesn't need grinding.

How are carnivore and herbivore teeth different?

The cat – a carnivore

The long, pointed **canines** are to catch animals.

The sharp **molars** work like scissors to cut meat up so it can be swallowed.

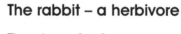

The rabbit – a herbivore

The sharp **incisors** are for nibbling on grass.

The wide **molars** grind it up to a soft pulp, ready for the stomach to digest it.

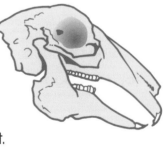

Herbivore	Carnivore
An animal that eats only plants.	An animal that eats only meat.

On track

1

wolf   sheep   cat   rabbit   horse   eagle

(a) Copy this table and fill it in to show what the different animals eat.

Carnivores (meat eaters)	Herbivores (plant eaters)
Wolf	

(b) What is the main difference between grass and meat that means herbivores and carnivores need different teeth?

A Grass is green.

B Grass is tougher than meat.

C Meat tastes nicer than grass.

Aiming higher

2   Ms O'Rourke showed Tiger class a sheep skull. They were interested in looking at the tops of the sheep's teeth. The ones in the side of the mouth were very wide and had very rough tops.

(a) What is the scientific name for the wide teeth found in the cheeks?

(b) Which sentence gives the best reason for the cheek teeth being so wide and rough?

A They are getting worn out.

B It makes them better at grinding up grass.

C The sheep could bite hard if it was frightened by a dog.

How well am I doing?

On track

I know that grass is much tougher than meat and has to be ground up before it can be digested.

Aiming higher

I can explain why carnivore molars are sharp and herbivore molars are wide.

6 What groups can we put animals into?

- Some kinds of animal have backbones and other kinds do not.
- We can split the animals with backbones into five main groups.

There are many different types of animal. All living things that can move around on their own are animals. Cats and dogs are animals, and so are people. Insects, snails and worms count as well. We can split animals up into smaller groups.

Which animals are invertebrates (do not have backbones)?

Snails and **slugs:** Very similar but snails have shells

Worms: bodies made of rings called segments.

Spiders: skeleton on the outside and eight legs

Insects: skeleton also on the outside and six legs

Which animals are vertebrates (have backbones)?

Fish have scales and fins and live in water.

Amphibians live on land but lay their eggs in water

Reptiles have scales, and lay eggs similar to birds.

The warm animals with hair or fur are **mammals**.

Birds are warm, have feathers and lay eggs. Most can fly.

Linnaeus (also called Carl von Linn)

He was a Swedish scientist who decided to give plants and animals names that show which groups they are in. His system is still used today.

On track

1 Here are the names of some animals. Some have backbones and some do not.

| human | worm | bee | robin | crab |
| spider | horse | frog | snail | goldfish |

(a) Copy out this table and put the names of the animals into the right list.

Vertebrates (with backbones)	Invertebrates (without backbones)

(b) Put some more rows on your table and add the names of some other animals.

Aiming higher

2 Here are some pairs of animals. They are alike in some ways and different in others.

| Pair 1 –
A reptile and
a bird |  | Pair 2 –
A fish and
a frog |  |
| Pair 3 –
A bird and
a mammal |  | Pair 4 –
A fish and
a reptile | |

Match up these sentences to the right pair of animals.

Which pair?	Description
	Both are warm but one has feathers.
	Both lay eggs on land but one has scales.
	Both lay eggs in the water but one can live on land.
	Both have scales but one lives in the water.

How well am I doing?

On track

I can name some animals that have backbones and some that do not.

Aiming higher

I can tell the differences between five types of animals with backbones.

7 What groups can we put plants into?

- Some kinds of plants have flowers, and other kinds do not.
- Plants with no flowers make seeds and spores without them.

The difference between flowering and non-flowering plants is easy – it is whether they have flowers or not! Most well known plants in the park or the garden have flowers, but not all of them. Pine tree don't have flowers – they have cones instead.

What are some flowering and non-flowering plants?

Flowering plants

Many flowers are brightly coloured, but grass flowers are small and green.

daffodil

grass

Non-flowering plants

Ferns and mosses don't have flowers, and neither do pine trees.

fern

pine

What difference does it make if a plant has flowers?

Flowers make **fruits**, which contain the **seeds** for next year.

The pips in an apple are its seeds.

The peas in a pea pod are seeds as well.

Non-flowering plants make seeds and spores in other ways.

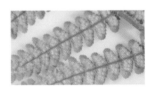

Underneath a fern leaf you can see the bumps where it makes its spores.

A pine tree's seeds are in the cone.

Seed

The part of a flower that will grow into next year's new plant.

Spore

Mosses and ferns make tiny spores instead of seeds.

On track

1 Tiger class have been looking for wild flowers. They have found lots of bluebells. Now they want to find some fern flowers. There are plenty of ferns, but there are no flowers on them.

(a) Explain why it isn't worth looking for fern flowers.

(b) What other kinds of non-flowering plants might they find in the wood?

(c) What could they collect from pine trees instead of flowers?

 Aiming higher

2 Squirrels eat pine cones. You can find lots of these left-over bits of cones underneath pine trees. The squirrels pull them to bits.

(a) What do you think the squirrel is trying to get to when she pulls them to bits?

(b) Squirrels also eat beech nuts and acorns from oak trees. These grow inside the flowers on those trees. What do the trees make these nuts for?

 How well am I doing?

On track

I can name some plants that have flowers and some that do not.

Aiming higher

I can explain what flowers are for, and how some plants manage without them.

8 How do you use a key?

- You can use a key to find out the name of an animal or a plant.
- You can make up your own keys.

Do you know the names of all the birds you see in the garden or at the park? It can take a long time to learn all the names. You can use a key to help. It is a way of finding the names by answering a few simple questions.

How does a key help us name plants and animals?

This key helps you find the names of these four birds. Answer the first question and follow the arrows to the next ones down. Those answers take you to the right names.

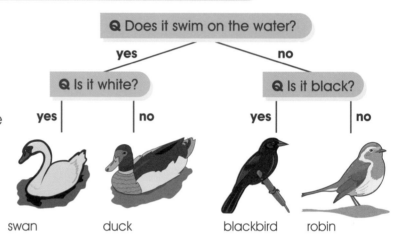

How do you make up your own questions for keys?

You can see that the key shown above works by asking questions that have simple yes or no answers.

- The first question splits the birds into two groups – ones that swim and ones that don't.
- The next row of questions is about the colours of the birds, and it takes you to the actual names.

If you wanted to ask a question that told the difference between a fish and a frog, you should ask about a feature you can easily see. You could ask "Has it got legs?"; yes for a frog, no for a fish.

Key

A way of setting out facts about plants and animals that tells you their names.

Features

Differences between things that let you tell them apart, like colour or shape.

On track

1 Jessica was collecting fruits and seeds. The picture shows the one she found.

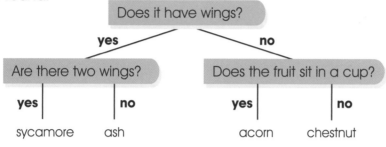

Does it have wings?

yes — Are there two wings?
no — Does the fruit sit in a cup?

Are there two wings?
yes | no
sycamore   ash

Does the fruit sit in a cup?
yes | no
acorn   chestnut

(a) What is the name of the one she found?

(b) Which fruit does not have any wings or a cup to hold the nut?

Aiming higher

1 Janek put together some facts about animals that live in England.

	What colour is its body?	Special features	What does it eat?
Fox	red/brown	bushy tail	rabbits
Badger	grey	striped face	fruit and small animals
Deer	sandy brown	males have antlers	grass
Rabbit	grey	long ears	grass

He made this key to identify the animals. Some parts are not filled in yet.

(a) What question could go in the space on the dotted line?

(b) What are the names of animals A, B and C?

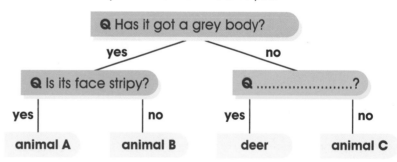

Q Has it got a grey body?
yes — no

Q Is its face stripy?
yes | no
animal A   animal B

Q ....?
yes | no
deer   animal C

How well am I doing?

On track

I can use a key to find the names of animals and plants.

Aiming higher

I can think of good questions to tell the difference between different sorts of plants and animals.

9 How do environments change?

- **The habitats of animals and plants are in danger of being spoiled.**
- **Humans cause a lot of the damage, but we can also do a lot to help.**

All sorts of things can change a habitat. Some are natural. If it rains a lot, a river might flood and fill up a field with water. All the mice, rabbits and foxes would have to go and live somewhere else. But the main thing spoiling habitats is … us!

How do people spoil habitats?

There are so many people in the world, and we all need somewhere to live. Over 8,000,000 (8 million) people live just in London. They take up a lot of space!

A great city like London has some very beautiful buildings, but they are all built where there was once wild countryside.

The habitats of the fish, forest animals and plants are gone forever.

How can we conserve the environment?

We can all do something to help.

We can all make sure we don't drop litter everywhere.

We can grow buddleia plants in the school garden. Butterflies love them!

Plant a tree! New forests can be made to bring back the wildlife.

Conservation
Keeping wild places in their natural state.

Deforestation
Clearing forests to grow food or build cities.

On track

1 More and more people are moving into the town where Ms O'Rourke's school is. Lots of new houses are being built for the people to live in.

(a) Why will building new homes in the town make it harder for owls to survive there?

(b) Out in the countryside the farmers are getting rid of their hedges to make their fields bigger. Why does that make it harder for owls to live?

Owls eat mice.

Aiming higher

2 Tiger class wanted to help the wildlife where they lived. Ms O'Rourke decided to let part of the school field go wild. It did not get mowed any more, and soon wild flowers and little bushes started to grow. Some of the children saw rabbits visiting the field, and in the evening a fox was seen.

(a) How did not mowing the grass help the rabbits?

(b) Why did the fox start visiting the school field?

How well am I doing?

On track

I can describe how wild habitats are sometimes spoiled by people.

Aiming higher

I can explain what we can do to look after wild habitats.

10 How are solids, liquids and gases different?

- Solids, liquids and gases have different properties.
- Some solids seem to act like a liquid because you can pour them.

All materials are **solids**, **liquids** or **gases** at room temperature. Solids like iron keep their shape. Liquids like water change their shape and can be poured. Gases are like air, have no shape and move to fill the space they are in. Solids with very small particles appear to pour just like a liquid. However, they are still in fact solids.

How are solids, liquids and gases different?

Solids:
- are hard
- difficult to compress
- keep their shape.

Liquids:
- pour and are runny
- take the shape of their container.

Gases:
- usually can't be seen
- fill their container
- escape from unsealed containers.

Why are some materials hard to group?

Grains of rice are hard. This makes you think rice is a solid. However, you can pour the grains into a bottle just like a liquid.

Most scientists agree rice is a solid because, although it pours, each grain is hard. It makes a pile and not a puddle! The same can be said of sand.

State of matter	Compress
Solids, liquids and gases are the three states of matter (materials).	To squeeze and squash together.

On track

1 Here are some everyday solids, liquids and gases.

petrol	ice	air	milk	helium	rice
blood	plastic	sand	chocolate	oxygen	iron

(a) Sort the twelve materials into three groups. Make one group of solids, one for liquids and one for gases.

(b) Add another two materials to each group.

2 Tiger class have poured 100 cm³ of water into four different shaped containers.

Which of these statements are **true**?

A   Water takes the shape of the container it is in.

B   The water will fill to the same level in each container.

C   Water is a solid.

Aiming higher

3 Mina was on the beach. She tipped some sand from her spade into her bucket.

(a) What might Mina see that made her think sand might be a liquid?

(b) What is it about sand that made her decide it was a solid?

(c) Can you name two other solids that can be poured?

How well am I doing?

On track

I can describe how solids, liquids and gases are different.

Aiming higher

I can explain why some materials are hard to group as solids or liquids.

11 What happens when you heat or cool water?

- Ice, water and water vapour are the three states of water.
- Heating or cooling water changes its state.

The water you drink is a liquid. Ice cubes are also water but in a solid form. Water vapour is the third state of water in the form of a gas. When water changes from one form into another, we say it is changing its state. Warming it up or cooling it down changes its state.

How can you change the state of water?

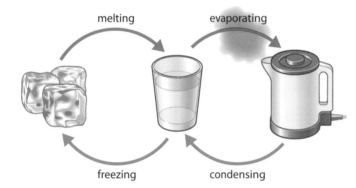

melting   evaporating

freezing   condensing

Warming solid ice makes it **melt** into water. Adding even more heat makes it **evaporate** into water vapour.

When water vapour is cooled, it **condenses** into water. If water is cooled, it **freezes** and becomes ice.

What are the three states of water?

Icebergs contain solid water.

Rain is water in its liquid form.

Clouds contain water vapour – a gas.

Condense

To change from a gas into a liquid: the opposite process to evaporating.

Freeze

To change from a liquid into a solid: the opposite process to melting.

On track

1   Ms O'Rourke asked Dominic and Kate to look at a boiling kettle.
    They could see water vapour coming out of the spout.

    (a) In what state is the water in while it is in the kettle? Pick one of these.

solid	liquid	gas

    (b) What is the state of water in the cloud of vapour?

    (c) Ice is made of water as well. What state is that in?

Aiming higher

2   Ms O'Rourke has lit a candle. Not
    many of the class use them these
    days. Candles have gone out of use.

    Her pupils notice that some of
    the wax runs down the side and
    becomes solid again.

    (a) What is the name of the process that turns the solid wax into a liquid?

    (b) What part of the candle makes this happen?

    (c) Explain why the wax has become a solid further down the candle.

How well am I doing?

On track

I can name the three states of water.

Aiming higher

I know how to name and describe the four
processes that change water between its
three states.

12 Can you predict how fast water heats up?

● **Patterns in data can help you make a prediction.**

● **You need to test to see if your prediction is correct.**

When water is heated it warms up. Everyone knows that. But does it do so in a regular way? You need to do a test to find this out. As scientists, you can put your results in a table or draw a graph to show how the temperature changes as it gets hotter. You may be able to see a pattern in the results.

Can you find a pattern in some data?

Ms O'Rourke tested what happens to the temperature of water as it is heated.

Time (minutes)	5	10	15	20	25	30	35	40
Temperature (°C)	20	25	30	36	40	45	50	55

Ms O'Rourke asked her class to look at this data and see if there was any pattern.

Most could see that the temperature rose by 5°C every five minutes. She challenged them to predict the next three results. Everyone said 60°C, 65°C and 70°C.

But would their predictions still be true if they heated the water for longer?

Does the pattern carry on forever?

Time (minutes)	65	70	75	80	85	90	95	40
Temperature (°C)	80	85	90	95	100	100	100	100

Ms O'Rourke gave them some more data. It showed the pattern was followed for a little while. But when the temperature of water reached 100°C, it stayed there.

It did so as long as it was still being heated. Ms O'Rourke said this was the boiling point of water.

Degrees Celsius

Units for measuring temperature invented by Anders Celsius in 1742. The scale used to be known as degrees centigrade (centum = 100, gradus = steps). This is the scale we use in our country.

On track

1 Ms O'Rourke heated the same amount of water. She did it slightly differently.
   Here are her results. It never boiled.

Time	2 minutes	4 minutes	6 minutes	8 minutes
Temperature	20	32	44	56

(a) What would the temperature be after three minutes?

(b) What would the temperature be after ten minutes?

(c) Did she heat the water more or less strongly? Explain your answer.

 Aiming higher

2 One group in Tiger class did another test. They heated up lemonade, which is water
   containing lots of sugar. Here are their results.

Time (minutes)	0	2	4	6	8	10	12	14
Temperature (°C)	20	40	60	80	100	103	103	103

(a) What temperature was room temperature?

(b) In the first eight minutes, how much does the temperature increase
    every minute?

(c) What is the boiling point of lemonade?

(d) What do you think will happen if the group takes the heat away from the
    boiling lemonade?

3 Draw a bar graph of Ms O'Rourke's first two experiments.

4 Draw a bar graph of Tiger class's experiment on heating up lemonade.

 How well am I doing?

On track

I can see a pattern in results and use them
to predict what might happen next.

Aiming higher

I can change my prediction if the results
are not what are expected.

13 What happens in the water cycle?

- Water continuously moves around the Earth in the water cycle.
- Changes of state such as evaporation and condensation help describe what happens to the water.

All over the world rivers run into the sea. So why doesn't the sea get deeper and deeper? What about the water in the rivers? Where does it come from? Will rivers ever dry up? Did dinosaurs once drink the same water as you? The answer to all these questions can be answered by understanding the **water cycle**.

What happens in the water cycle?

The same water continually goes around and around in the water cycle, just like in the diagram.

In other places the water cycle might be more complicated, depending on the seasons and the geography of the ground.

What changes of state occur in the water cycle?

Evaporation occurs when liquid water warms up and changes into water vapour in the air.

Condensation occurs when water vapour cools down and turns into liquid water like rain.

Freezing occurs when liquid water cools down enough to turn into solid water like snow or ice.

Melting occurs when solid water like ice warms up enough to change into liquid water.

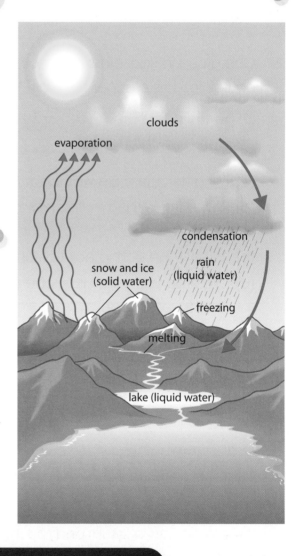

clouds

evaporation

condensation

rain
(liquid water)

snow and ice
(solid water)

freezing

melting

lake (liquid water)

0 °C

The temperature at which water freezes or melts.

Continually

Something that happens time and time again.

On track

1 This drawing shows part of a
   water cycle.

   (a) The Sun evaporates some
        water from the sea. What
        keeps it topped up?

   (b) Water keeps on flowing to the
        sea. What keeps the streams
        from drying up?

   (c) Where do the clouds get
        their water from?

   (d) Explain why you might have drunk some water that a dinosaur once drank.

Aiming higher

2 This diagram shows where water changes its state in the water cycle..

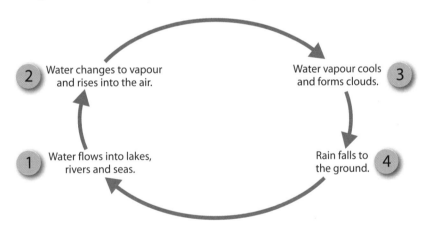

   (a) At which stage (1–4) does evaporation take place?

   (b) At which stage (1–4) does condensation take place?

   (c) What might happen to the rain if it were very cold?

How well am I doing?

On track

I can describe what happens in the water
cycle.

Aiming higher

I can use the idea of a change of state to
explain how the water cycle works.

14 What affects how fast ice melts?

- Warming up solid ice melts it into liquid water.
- The temperature of the room affects how fast ice melts.

When ice warms up in a room it changes into liquid water. This happens at 0°C. The temperature of ice stays at 0°C until it all melts. Then the cold water warms up to the temperature of the room. The warmer the room, the faster the ice will melt.

What did Jaldev see when he let some ice warm up?

Jaldev put some ice cubes in water. He left this in his classroom and took the temperature of the mixture every five minutes. He then drew a graph of his results.

A   The temperature is below 0°C. The ice slowly warms up.

B   The temperature stays at 0°C (the melting point of ice) until all the ice melts.

C   The water slowly warms up.

D   Eventually the temperature of the water settles at room temperature, 22°C.

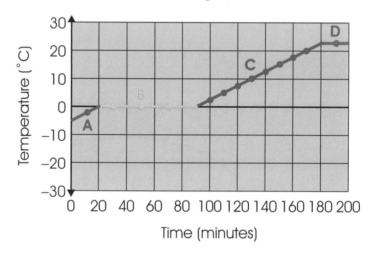

What affects how fast ice melts?

Ice melts because it takes heat from the room. What if the room was warmer to start with? Would a warm room make the ice melt faster than it would in a cold room? This table of results shows us the answer.

The warmer the room, the faster the ice melted.

Temperature of the room	Time taken to melt an ice cube
18°C	10 minutes
20°C	8 minutes
22°C	6 minutes

Room temperature
The normal temperature of a room.

Table
A good way of organising results.

RISING ★ STARS

Science Study Guide: Year 4

Answer Booklet

Unit		On track		Aiming higher	
1 What teeth have you got?	**1 (a)**	A suitable chart | **My teeth**	**Top row**	**Bottom row** | |---|---|---| | Incisors | 4 | 4 | | Canines | 2 | 2 | | Molars | 4 | 4 | | **Total** | 10 | 10 |	**2 (a)**		Name of tooth	Main job of tooth | |---|---| | Incisor | B | | Canine | C | | Molar | A |	
	(b) **(c)**	Full set of milk teeth 20. *Own answers*	**(b)**	They are sharp and pointed.	
2 How can you look after your teeth?	**1 (a)** **(b)** **(c)**	Milk teeth Two You need a bigger set for a bigger mouth.	**2 (a)** **(b)**	Avoid sugary drinks that feed the germs that rot teeth. Eat apples and carrots because they don't feed the germs. Brushing teeth cleans off the germs that rot teeth.	
3 What is your digestive system?	**1**		Description	Body part	 |---|---| | Where the teeth and tongue are found. | Mouth | | Grind up food until its soft for swallowing. | Teeth | | A long tube connecting the stomach to the bottom. | Intestine | | Takes food from the mouth to the stomach. | Oesophagus | | Helps us swallow our food, and also to taste it. | Tongue | | A bag that holds the food. Some digestion happens here. | Stomach |	**2**	In the mouth: chewing In the oesophagus: food passed along to stomach In the stomach: food and drink mixed up In the intestine (1): digestive juices finish digestion In the intestine (2): Dissolved food carried away by blood.	
4 What are food chains?	**1**		Predator	Prey	Producer	 |---|---|---| | Cat | Mouse | Wheat | | Wolf | Sheep | Grass |	**2 (a)** **(b)** **(c)**	Leaves → caterpillar → thrush → owl Producer – leaves Predators – thrush, owl Prey – thrush, caterpillar Grass → sheep → wolf Wheat → mouse → cat	
5 Do animals that eat different foods have different teeth?	**1 (a)** **(b)**		Carnivores	Herbivores	 |---|---| | Wolf | Sheep | | Cat | Rabbit | | Eagle | Horse | B – Grass is tougher than meat	**2 (a)** **(b)**	Molars B – It makes them better at grinding up grass	

Unit		On track			Aiming higher

6 What groups can we put animals into?	1 (a)			2	

Unit 6 — What groups can we put animals into?

1 (a)

With backbones	Without backbones
Human	Worm
Robin	Bee
Horse	Crab
Frog	Spider
Goldfish	Snail

(b) *Own answers*

2

Which pair	Description
Pair 1	Both lay eggs on land but one has scales
Pair 2	Both lay eggs in the water but one can live on land
Pair 3	Both are warm but one has feathers
Pair 4	Both have scales but one lives in the water

7 What groups can we put plants into?

On track
1 (a) Ferns don't have flowers
(b) Pine trees
(c) Pine cones

Aiming higher
2 (a) The pine seeds
(b) They are seeds to grow into new plants

8 How do you use a key?

On track
1 (a) Sycamore
(b) Chestnut

Aiming higher
2 (a) Does it eat grass?
(b) Animal A: badger
Animal B: rabbit
Animal C: fox

9 How do environments change?

On track
1 (a) It destroys habitat. There is nowhere for owls to nest or hunt.
(b) The mice and small animals that owls hunt live in hedgerows.

Aiming higher
2 (a) There was more grass for the rabbits to eat.
(b) The fox was hunting the rabbits.

10 How are solids, liquids and gases different?

On track
1 (a) Solids: ice, rice, plastic, sand, chocolate, iron
Liquids: petrol, milk, blood
Gases: air, helium, oxygen
(b) *Own answers*
2 A – Water takes the shape of the container it is in.

Aiming higher
3 (a) It poured.
(b) The individual particles of sand are hard. They keep their shape and cannot be squashed.
(c) Answers can include: flour, salt and rice.

11 What happens when you heat or cool water?

On track
1 (a) Liquid
(b) Gas
(c) Solid

Aiming higher
2 (a) Melting
(b) The flame
(c) The wax has cooled down and condensed.

12 Can you predict how fast water heats up?

On track
1 (a) 26°C
(b) 68°C
(c) More strongly. It is warming by 6°C per minute; in the earlier test it was 1°C per minute.

Aiming higher
2 (a) 20°C
(b) 10°C per minute
(c) 103°C
(d) It will start to cool down
3 A suitable graph
4 A suitable graph

13 What happens in the water cycle?

On track
1 (a) The rivers flowing into it.
(b) Rain refills the streams
(c) Evaporation from the sea and rivers.
(d) It is all the same water being endlessly recycled.

Aiming higher
2 (a) Stage 2
(b) Stage 3
(c) It could freeze to sleet or hail.

14 What affects how ice melts?

On track
1 (a) 30°C
(b) The hotter room makes the ice melt faster and the water heats up to room temperature faster.

Aiming higher
2 (a) Classroom 3
(b) I think a warmer classroom will melt ice faster because it can give more heat to melt the ice.

15 What is evaporation?

On track
1 (a) A suitable graph
(b) 11.00 am.
(c) It is evaporating into the air.

Aiming higher
2 (a) Olive oil – paintbrush cleaner – vinegar – water

16 What makes water evaporate faster?

On track
1 (a) B – The warmer the room, the faster the water evaporates.
(b) She would need a beaker, something to measure water with, a thermometer, water and rooms of different temperatures.
(c) The temperature of the room.
(d) The amount of water she starts with/ the temperature of the water at the start.
(e) The time it takes for all the water to evaporate.

Aiming higher
2 (a) The warmer the room the faster the water evaporates
(b) Repeat the tests in each room several times – then take an average of each set of results.

Unit		On track		Aiming higher
17 What are melting points?	**1 (a)**	Melting	**2 (a)**	Metal spoon and gold ring: both are made of metal. Metals generally have higher melting points.
	(b)	Chocolate has a melting point just below the temperature of Ali's mouth.		
	(c)	Both melted, the lolly much faster.	**(b)**	Butter and chocolate.
	(d)	0°C		
18 Where do sounds come from?	**1**	*Own answers*	**3 (a)**	His larynx
	2 (a)	Loud, shrill, low	**(b)**	Vibrations travel along the string to the other can, then through the air to Annette.
	(b)	Answers can include: The jet engine was very loud. The bird song was shrill. The man sang a very low note.	**(c)**	Sound travels best through a solid.
19 How do stringed instruments work?	**1 (a)**	String and body of guitar vibrate	**2 (a)**	The thickest band has a lower note.
	(b)	Pluck the strings gently.	**(b)**	The shorter string has a higher note.
	(c)	Pluck the strings harder.	**(c)**	Use a shorter length of thick string to sound higher.
	2	*Own answers*		
	3	Having a bigger soundboard or soundbox.		
20 How do wind instruments work?	**1**	*Own answers*	**3 (a)**	Air
	2 (a)	The column of air in the tube	**(b)**	D
	(b)	Blow harder	**(c)**	A
	(c)	Cover up more or less holes	**(d)**	The smaller the air volume, the higher the pitch of the note.
21 How do percussion instruments work?	**1**	*Own answers*	**3 (a)**	
	2 (a)	The drum skin		
	(b)	C, B, A, D (D is lowest)		
	(c)	Sound can travel through the air and through the floor		

3 (a)

How you play the drum	The sound ...
Tighter drum skin	higher note
Hit harder	louder note
Hit drum faster	no difference to the note

Unit		On track		Aiming higher
22 Which fair test on sound is better?	**1 (a)**	Sounds get fainter as the distance from the sound source increases.	**2 (a)**	The loudness decreased as the distance increased.
	(b)	Harry and Cerys Keep the same: how hard they clapped hands. Change: distance of observer from clapping. Mohammed and Nina Keep the same: note loudness from horn. Change: distance of observer from sound.	**(b)**	The same
			(c)	A suitable graph
			(d)	No, verbal descriptions cannot be set on a numerical scale.
	(c)	Harry and Cerys: handclap. Mohammed and Nina: horn.	**(e)**	Second test is better scientifically. Better control over variables, numerical results recorded using instrumentation, not subjective impression.
	(d)	The horn was better because it has a more reliable constant sound.		
23 What materials muffle sounds best?	**1 (a)**	Apparatus used: different materials (newspaper, fur, cotton wool), buzzer that works by itself, box, sound meter.	**2 (a)**	Fur, screwed-up newspaper, cotton wool. No.
	(b)	The box, the amount of material, the distance the sound meter is away from the box, the buzzer.	**(b)**	dB or decibels
	(c)	The loudness of sound.	**(c)**	To repeat their measurements several times and take an average of their results
	(d)	The material inside the box.		
	(e)	To see how loud the buzzer is without any material, so they could see the effect each material has on the loudness of the sound.		

Unit		On track		Aiming higher
24 What do we use electricity for?	1 (a) (b)	A suitable table Answers can include: no heating, cooking, refrigeration and lighting, as well as having no TV or games!	2 (a) (b)	Danger 1 – The man standing on the table could fall off if it tips over./Use a ladder. Danger 2 – The boy is playing with screwdriver in a live plug socket./Use a socket cover. Danger 3 – The vase of flowers on top of the TV could fall and cause short circuits./Move vase to a table. Danger 4 – The cable is stretched and lamp could fall on the baby./Make sure cables are neat and tidy. Danger 5 – The girl poking the electric fire could be burned or get an electric shock./Use a fire grate. 1: Conduction of electricity where not wanted. 2: Avoids fire hazard of overloading cable 3: Tripping and frayed cables 4: Electricity can pass through human tissue 5: Greater experience to identify hazards 6: Limited awareness of hazards
25 What components are used in circuits?	1 (a) (b)	Cell: Provides electricity Switch: Turns circuit on or off Wire: Joins the components together Motor: Provides electricity Buzzer: Makes a noise Lamp: Lights up Battery: Provides more electricity A battery is a row of two or more cells joined and working together	2	Circuit diagrams as appropriate, using symbols as shown opposite.
26 What do you need for an electrical circuit to work?	1 (a) (b) (c)	Cells provide power/produce electricity Turn one cell around A	2 (a) (b) 3	One cell wrong way round; plastic spoon cannot conduct electricity. One cell turned; no plastic spoon – end joined to give complete circuit. Circuit drawn correctly.
27 What kinds of material conduct electricity?	1 (a) (b) (c)	Metal core To stop electricity reaching you. Tanya could put some of the wire coating into the testing circuit. It will not conduct electricity.	2 (a) (b)	Conductors: key, ring pull, gold ring Insulators: feather, stone. Own answers
28 How do switches work?	1 (a) (b)	On/off switches on radio, phone, torch, TV, mp3 player To save power/to stop the battery running out.	2 (a) (b) (c) (d)	Nothing The bulb will light. Completes circuit/allows electricity to flow. No – wood is an insulator

Unit 29

29 What makes bulbs brighter or dimmer in a circuit?

1 (a) Does changing the number of bulbs in a circuit affect how brightly they light up?

(b)

	Kept the same	Changed	Observed
Number of bulbs		✓	
type of bulb	✓		
number of cells	✓		
brightness of bulb(s)			✓

2 (a)

	Kept the same	Changed	Observed
Number of bulbs	✓		
type of bulb	✓		
number of cells		✓	
brightness of bulb(s)			✓

(b) Suitable circuits drawn using the correct symbols or drawings.

(c) Circuits correctly labelled.

 On track

1   Jaldev then did a second
    test. He put a similar ice/water
    mixture into a much warmer
    room.

    Again he took the temperature
    of the water every five minutes.

    Here is the second graph he
    drew.

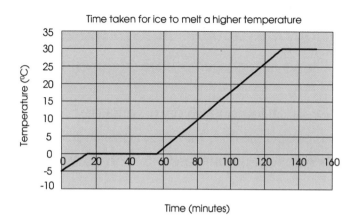

Time taken for ice to melt a higher temperature

Temperature (°C) vs Time (minutes)

(a) What is the room temperature in this second room?

(b) Describe the difference the temperature in the second room has on the time
     taken for the ice/water mixture to warm up.

 Aiming higher

2   Jaldev did a third test. He wanted to find the warmest classroom in the school.

    He gave each class the
    same-sized ice cube on
    a plate. Each class
    measured how long
    it took to melt.

Classroom	Time taken for the ice cube to melt
3	25 mins
4	30 mins
5	42 mins
6	28 mins

(a) Look at his results. Which classroom was the warmest?

(b) Describe how the temperature of the room affects the time taken for the ice
     cube to melt. Try using an "I think … because …" sentence.

 How well am I doing?

On track

I can describe what happens when ice
melts and warms up.

Aiming higher

I can explain why an ice cube melts faster
in a warm room.

15 What is evaporation?

- **Liquids evaporate to form gases.**
- **Some liquids evaporate faster at room temperature than others.**

Any liquid left to stand will dry up after a while. This is because it has evaporated. When liquids evaporate they turn into a gas and often go into the air. Liquids with low boiling points evaporate faster than those with high boiling points.

What is evaporation?

Jolie noticed that all liquids dry out. For example, puddles of water seem to dry up. But the water has not really gone away; it has just changed into water vapour and gone into the air.

Perfume is the same. As it evaporates, the gas spreads out into the room. The air carries it to you.

How fast do liquids evaporate?

Washing hung up outside on the line could take a few hours to dry. It is much quicker in a tumble drier. The higher the temperature outside, the faster the water evaporates.

Not only water evaporates. Perfume evaporates faster than water because its boiling point is much lower.

Evaporate

When a liquid turns into a gas.

Water vapour

The proper name for the gas that liquid water turns into.

 On track

1   Jolie measured a puddle in the playground. The rain had stopped and the puddle was drying up in the sunshine. She then measured the puddle every half an hour.

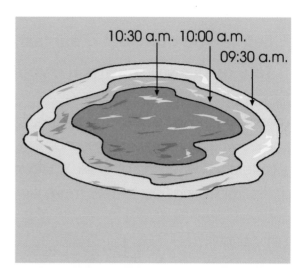

Time	Size of puddle
9:30	280 cm
10:00	140 cm
10:30	70 cm

(a) Draw a bar chart to show how the puddle changed size.

(b) At what time do you think the puddle might have disappeared altogether?

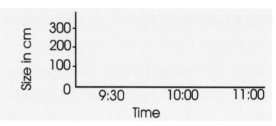

(c) What was happening to the water to explain why the puddle was drying up?

 Aiming higher

2   Jolie looked up the boiling points of some household liquids on the Internet.

(a) List the liquids in the table in the order of how fast they evaporate at room temperature. Start with the slowest first.

Liquid	Boiling point
water	100°C
paintbrush cleaner	160°C
olive oil	300°C
vinegar	118°C

 How well am I doing?

On track

I can explain what evaporation is.

Aiming higher

I can describe the link between boiling point and speed of evaporation.

16 What makes water evaporate faster?

- **Before you carry out a fair test, it is best to make a prediction.**
- **Your results will show you if your prediction was a good one.**

Water can evaporate at different rates. For example, puddles disappear more quickly in summer, when the air is warmer, than in winter. If a breeze blows across a puddle it will dry faster than when the air is still. You can find out if your ideas are true by carrying out a fair test. Repeating your test will make it more reliable!

How did Finley test his prediction?

Finley predicted that "the more a container is open to the air, the faster water will evaporate".

To test this he used four beakers that were the same size. Each contained $100\,cm^3$ of water. A piece of cardboard covered each beaker, but the four pieces of cardboard had different sized holes in them. The beakers were left for 4 hours. Finally, the volume of water was recorded at the end to work out the volume that had evaporated.

What did his results tell him?

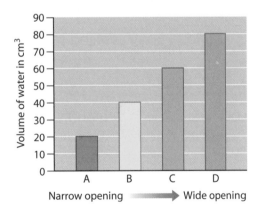

Look carefully at Finley's results on his bar chart.

In the beaker with the narrowest openings, only $20\,cm^3$ of water had evaporated. In the beaker with the widest openings, $80\,cm^3$ of water had evaporated.

Finley's prediction was right! The wider the openings in the cardboard, the faster the water evaporates. This is because the wider opening lets more air blow by, which quickens the rate of evaporation.

Results

The measurements you make in a fair test.

Bar chart

A chart with rectangular bars whose size tells you the value of what was measured.

On track

1 Malika wanted to test to see if the temperature of the room made a difference to how fast water evaporated.

(a) Which of these predictions is most likely to turn out right in the end?

   A "The colder the room, the faster the water evaporates."

   B "The warmer the room, the faster the water evaporates."

   C "The temperature makes no difference to how fast water evaporates."

(b) What equipment would she need to do her fair test?

(c) What should she change as she carries out her test?

(d) What should she keep the same to make her test fair?

(e) What should she measure to collect her results?

Aiming higher

2 Malika did her test and put her results in a table.

Classroom	Temperature of the room	Volume of water that evaporated after six hours
3	22°C	20 cm³
4	25°C	25 cm³
5	35°C	45 cm³
6	30°C	30 cm³

(a) Use the pattern in her results to say which prediction turned out to be true.

(b) What would you ask her to do to make her results more reliable?

How well am I doing?

On track

I can come up with sensible predictions to test.

Aiming higher

I can say whether the results of a test support the predictions.

17 What are melting points?

- Solids change into liquids at a temperature called the **melting point**.
- Different materials have different melting points.

Solids change into liquids when heated. This process is called melting.
Some solids melt at very low temperatures. Others, such as metals, melt at very high temperatures. Liquids freeze into solids when they are cooled.

What happens at melting points?

Chocolate is usually solid, but if you warm it up it will melt to a liquid.

Chocolate is made to melt just above 36°C. This means it melts in your mouth.

How different are melting points?

Metals such as gold melt at high temperatures. Gold melts into a liquid at over 1000°C.

Candle wax melts at around 150°C. A hot flame will melt it.

Butter melts between 30°C–35°C. On most days in Britain it is solid, but it will melt on a very hot day.

Solid water is called ice. Ice changes to liquid water when it is heated above 0°C. It freezes to ice when cooled below 0°C.

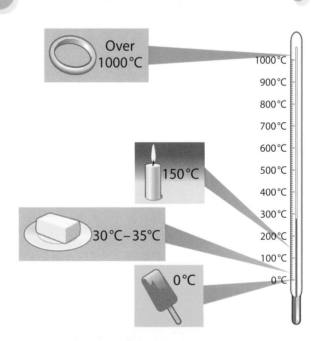

Over 1000°C

150°C

30°C–35°C

0°C

| 1000°C |
| 900°C |
| 800°C |
| 700°C |
| 600°C |
| 500°C |
| 400°C |
| 300°C |
| 200°C |
| 100°C |
| 0°C |

Melting point

The temperature at which a solid changes into its liquid.

Freezing point

The temperature at which a liquid changes into its solid.

On track

1   Ali had an ice lolly and some chocolate to eat. It was 30°C outside and very warm.

   (a) What is the name given to the process when Ali's lolly and chocolate change from a solid into a liquid?

   (b) Ali ate a piece of chocolate. Explain why it melted in his mouth.

   (c) Ali left the lolly and chocolate on the table. What happened to them?

   (d) Ali put his lolly into a freezer. What should the temperature be so that it stays solid?

Aiming higher

2   Ali had four different materials. He wondered at what temperature they would melt.

Butter	Iron	Chocolate	Gold

   (a) Which two materials have the highest melting points? Explain your answer.

   (b) Which materials would melt on a hot day?

How well am I doing?

On track

I can explain what the words "melting point" mean.

Aiming higher

I can name some materials that melt at very high temperatures.

18 Where do sounds come from?

- There are many different sources of sound.
- You hear a sound when it enters your ear.

Your ears detect the sounds around you. You hear many different sounds every day. Have you ever wondered how they are made? There are many different sources of sound. Sounds can travel through solids, liquids or gases.

Where do sounds come from?

People, animals, nature, machines and musical instruments are sources of sound. Each one sounds different.

Thunder makes a deep rumbling sound.

Each guitar string has a different note.

Everyone's singing voice is different.

Some engines can be very loud.

How do you hear the sounds?

Before sounds enter your ears, they have to travel through solids and liquids or gases. They travel quickest through solids and slowest through gases such as air.

Harry hears sounds that travel through water.

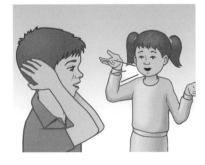
The sound of singing travels through air to his ears.

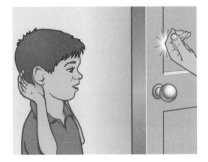
Before the knocking sound enters his ears, it travels through solids and air.

Source
The point where something starts or originates from.

Sound
A form of energy that is detected by your ears.

On track

1 Ms O'Rourke asked Tiger class to think of different sources of sound and put them in a table. Some pupils added sources that were not in the classroom.

Sound	What makes the sound?	Extra facts
Ms O'Rourke's voice	Her voice box (larynx) in her throat	Your ears can tell it apart from other voices.
School bell		

(a) Make a table like the one above. Fill it in with as many sources as you can.

2 Look at these words.

loud	heavy	shrill	cool	low	smelly

(a) Three of these words can be used to describe sounds. Which ones?

(b) Use each word in a sentence to show how it is used correctly.

Aiming higher

3

(a) What vibrates when Jaldev speaks?

(b) Explain how Annetta hears Jaldev speaking through the telephone.

(c) Which of these statements is true?

    A Sound cannot travel through a solid.

    B Sound travels faster through a gas than a liquid.

    C Sound travels best through a solid.

How well am I doing?

On track

I can name at least ten different sources of sound.

Aiming higher

I can describe how different sounds travel from a source to our ears.

19 How do stringed instruments work?

- Sounds are made when strings vibrate.
- You can change the loudness and pitch which the strings make.

Guitars are stringed instruments. When you pluck the strings they vibrate and a sound is made. This makes the rest of the guitar vibrate. The soundboard and a sound box make the sound even louder. Big or small vibrations produce loud or quiet sounds. Fast or slow vibrations produce high-pitched or low-pitched sounds.

How do you change the volume of the notes?

If you pluck the strings gently, the sound is quiet. This is because the vibrations are quite small.

If you pluck the strings harder, the sound gets louder. This is because the vibrations are bigger.

How do you change the pitch of each note?

A bird sings with a high-pitched note; a lorry's engine has a low-pitched note. A guitar can produce both high- and low-pitched notes.

The shorter the length of the vibrating strings, the higher the note's pitch. Longer length vibrations make low notes.

Shortening the string by pressing down on the frets alters the pitch. The pitch gets higher as you move up the fret board.

Plucking different strings also alters the pitch. Thick strings make a lower pitched note than thin strings of the same length.

Volume

How loud a sound is.

Pitch

Describes how high or low a note sounds.

On track

1   Sam is playing his guitar for the first time. He is finding out about the sounds it can make. He looks carefully at the strings when he plucks them.

   (a) Name two things that vibrate when he plucks a string.

   (b) What would he do to make a quiet sound?

   (c) How would he make the sound louder?

2   Name five instruments that work by plucking strings.

3   What makes the sound louder in a stringed instrument?

 Aiming higher

2   Sam has made a toy guitar out of a shoebox and four elastic bands. Each elastic band is the same length but a different thickness.

   (a) How is the sound of the thickest band different from the thinnest one?

   (b) Sam shortens one string by equal amounts using the frets. What happens to the sound of the note as he does so?

   (c) How would you make the thickest string sound the same as the thinnest string? What do the soundboard and sound box do to the sound?

 How well am I doing?

On track

I can explain how to change the volume of a note in a stringed instrument.

Aiming higher

I can explain how to change the pitch of a note in a stringed instrument.

20 How do wind instruments work?

- Sounds can be made by making air vibrate.
- Wind instruments can make high or low pitched notes.

Trumpets, trombones, recorders, clarinets and other wind instruments are basically long tubes of air. They make a sound when you blow into them, making the air vibrate. The harder you blow, the louder the sound. The shorter you make the length of air, the higher the pitch of the note.

How does a wind instrument work?

You play brass instruments like the trumpet and trombone by blowing through your lips into the mouthpiece.

A clarinet has a reed in the mouthpiece that buzzes when you blow.

It is this blowing or buzzing that starts the air vibrating so the instrument makes its sound.

The harder you blow into these instruments, the louder the sound.

How do you change the pitch of a recorder note?

The length of the column of air inside a recorder can change. You do this by closing up the holes with your fingers. The lowest pitched note is made when all the holes are covered and there is a long column of air. The highest note is made when no holes are covered and the air column is much shorter. The rule is: the longer the column of vibrating air, the lower the pitch of the note!

Rule	Note
A pattern that can be used in different situations.	A musical note of a certain pitch.

On track

1   Name five wind instruments.

2   Lots of pupils in Tiger class play the recorder.

   (a) What vibrates in a recorder to make the sound?

   (b) How do you make the sound louder?

   (c) Explain how you make the pitch of the note higher or lower.

Aiming higher

3   Pupils from Tiger class are testing the sounds that are made by four bottles. Each bottle is the same but contains a different amount of water.

They blew across each one in turn.

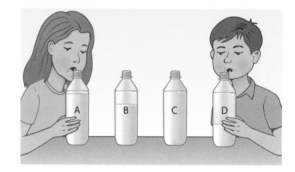

   (a) What vibrates when they blow into the bottles?

   (b) Which bottle (A–D) would make the lowest pitched sound?

   (c) Which bottle (A–D) would make the highest pitched sound?

   (d) Write down the rule that describes what makes the pitch get higher.

How well am I doing?

On track

I can explain how to change the volume and pitch of wind instruments.

Aiming higher

I can describe a rule that will tell me what makes the pitch get higher.

21 How do percussion instruments work?

● Sounds can be made by making skins, bells or wooden bars vibrate.

● Each instrument has its own pitch, but this can be changed.

Drums, bells, cymbals and xylophones are all percussion instruments. When you hit a drum, the skin vibrates, and this makes the rest of the drum vibrate. The sound travels to you through the air or through the floor and your body.

Can you show vibrations on a drum skin?

One group tested drum sounds. The drum skin had rice on it. As they tapped the skin it vibrated and the rice jumped up and down.

The harder they tapped the skin, the bigger were the vibrations and the louder the sound. The pitch of the note stayed the same.

They did the same with a smaller drum. This had a higher pitch. Their rule was "the bigger the drum, the lower the pitch of the note".

What makes a percussion instrument have a higher pitch?

Each individual part of a percussion instrument has its own note. You have to play more than one note to play a tune with different pitched notes.

The smaller the handbell, the higher the pitch.

The longer the bar, the lower the pitch.

The larger the cymbal, the lower the pitch.

Alexander Graham Bell

Alexander Graham Bell (1847–1922): an Scottish-born American scientist who invented the telephone. He gave his name to the units, decibels (dB), that measure the volume of sound. On this scale a whisper is 15 dB and normal conversation is 60 dB.

On track

1   Name five percussion instruments.

2   Tiger class have a drum kit. The skins are the same tightness but they are all of different sizes.

   (a) What vibrates when you tap each drum with a stick?

   (b) Put the drums in order (A to D) of the notes they make. Put the lowest pitched drum first.

   (c) Explain two ways the sound of a drum travels to your ears.

Aiming higher

3   Tiger class can change the way they play the drums. They can make the sound get louder or higher.

   (a) Copy the table. Tick **one** box in each row to show if the sound will get higher or lower.

How you play the drum	The sound ...		
	gets higher	gets louder	does not get higher or louder
With a tighter drum skin			
Hit the drum with the same force			
Hit the drum faster with the same force			

How well am I doing?

On track

I can explain how to change the volume of a percussion instrument.

Aiming higher

I can explain how to make different pitched notes on percussion instruments.

22 Which fair test on sound is better?

- You can test a scientific prediction to see if it is true.
- Some tests are scientifically better than others.

Tiger class decided to test their prediction that "sounds get fainter as the distance from the sound source increases". Two groups came up with their own tests. Although they were similar in some ways, the tests were different in other ways. Which one do you think was better?

How did Harry and Cerys do their test?

Harry stands on one spot so he can see Cerys. She claps her hands once – as loud as she can. Harry writes how loud the sound was using everyday words.

Cerys walks away, counting the number of steps away from Harry. She claps again. Harry writes the second result.

Cerys does this several times more, doubling the number of steps each time.

How did Mohammed and Nina do their test?

Nina stands next to Mohammed. She has a horn which makes the same loud noise when she blows it. Mohammed measures how loud the sound is in decibels (dB). He has a special machine to do this.

Nina uses a long tape measure and walks 25 m away. She sounds the horn again. Mohammed takes a second reading.

She repeats this, doubling the distance in metres, every time she does it.

Fair test

A scientific test where only one factor is changed.

Accurate

Something that is done with precision in the best way you can.

On track

1 Think about how the two groups planned and carried out their tests.

(a) What was the prediction they were testing?

(b) What did each group keep the same? What did they change? What did they measure in their test? Put your answer in a table – do one for each group.

(c) What did each group use as their sound source? Was one better than the other? If so, write a sentence to say why.

(d) What did each group use to measure the sound level? Was one better than the other? If so, write a sentence to say why.

Aiming higher

2 Here are the results from the two groups.

Number of steps between Harry and Cerys	The sound Harry hears	Distance between Mohammed and Nina (m)	The loudness of the sound (dB)
1 step	Extremely loud	1	69
25 steps	Very loud	25	41
50 steps	Loud	50	35
100 steps	Quieter	100	28
200 steps	Very quiet	200	22
400 steps	Nothing	400	16

(a) What does the table tell you about how the loudness of the sound changes in the two tests?

(b) Is the basic finding (result) the same or different?

(c) Draw a bar chart of Harry and Cerys's results.

(d) Can you do the same for Mohammed and Nina's results?

(e) Which of the two tests is scientifically better? Explain your answer.

How well am I doing?

On track

I know what to keep the same, change and measure in a fair test.

Aiming higher

I can explain what might make a fair test better.

23 What materials muffle sounds best?

- Fair tests help you see which materials muffle sound best.
- Test results help prove or disprove your predictions.

Have you noticed how the same sound differs from room to room? Soft materials in your house such as carpets or curtains **muffle** or absorb the sound. What is a loud sound in one room might not be in another. You can test to see which materials do this well.

How did Tiger class plan their fair test?

Tiger class wanted to test "which materials muffled sound best?"

They put a loud buzzer in a box. It was switched on from outside the box. On top of the box was a sound meter. This could measure the loudness of the buzzer inside the box.

First of all they measured the loudness of the buzzer in the box with nothing else in it. Then they put different materials in the box, one at a time, and measured the loudness of the buzzer again.

Tiger class tested three materials: **newspaper**, **fur** and **cotton wool**.

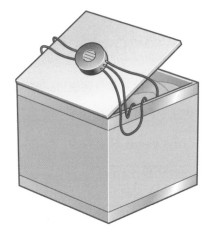

A sound meter measures the loudness of the sound in decibels (dB).

What predictions did they make?

"The newspaper will not be very good because it is too thin."

"Fur will be very good because it is used in ear muffs."

"Cotton wool will be good because it is very soft."

The class thought fur would be the best and newspaper the worst at stopping sound getting out of the box. Their results would help them find out which prediction was best.

Muffle

To absorb or soak up sounds and make them sound fainter

Sound insulator

A material that reduces or stops sound passing through it.

On track

1 Think about how Tiger class planned and thought about their investigation.

    (a) Make a list of all the apparatus they used.

    (b) What factors do they keep the same in the test?

    (c) What did they measure in their test?

    (d) What factor do they change in the test?

    (e) Explain why the class did the first test without any other materials in the box.

Aiming higher

2 Tiger class made a table of their results.

Type of insulating material	Sound level (dB)
No insulating material	65
Cotton wool	44
Fur	28
Screwed-up newspaper	34

    (a) Put the materials in the order of the best sound insulators. Put the best first and the worst last. Did the results turn out as the pupils predicted?

    (b) What units are being used to measure the sound level?

    (c) What would you ask the pupils to do to make their results more reliable?

How well am I doing?

On track

I can describe how to set up a fair test.

Aiming higher

I can say whether test results prove or disprove a prediction.

24 What do we use electricity for?

- **Many everyday appliances use electricity.**
- **Electricity can be very dangerous: you have to use it safely.**

Nearly every house in our country has electricity. A small number of houses in very rural areas still do not have it. Many appliances you use run on batteries or mains electricity. Remembering safety rules can stop accidents with electricity.

What makes electricity useful?

Electricity is available at the turn of a switch, 24 hours a day. It is affordable, if you use it sensibly, even though prices are rising.

Many years ago people did not have electricity in their homes. They used wax candles to give them light and burned wood in their cookers. Coal fires kept them warm.

Today mobile phones, televisions, water heaters, cookers, electric motors, cars and light bulbs all use electricity. Many people would find it hard to live without them.

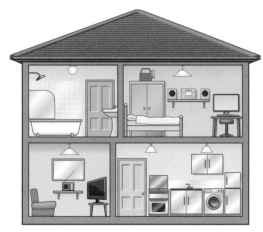

Every room in this house uses electricity.

How to keep safe with electricity?

Electricity can be dangerous. It can give you an electrical shock, cause a fire, ruin appliances and even kill you. These **rules** will help you keep safe.

1 Keep appliances away from water.

2 Don't put more than one plug into a wall socket.

3 Make sure all electrical cables are neat and tidy.

4 Do not put your fingers or other objects into appliances or sockets.

5 Never use appliances unless an adult says it is safe.

6 Keep small children away from anything electrical.

Plug and socket

Devices that connect electricity to your appliances. The first plugs and sockets were introduced in England in 1883 by T.T. Smith.
The ones you use today are much improved and safer to use.

On track

1   Ms O'Rourke gave her class some homework. She asked them to research the appliances they had in each room of their houses.

Rooms in my house	Appliances in each room that use batteries	Appliances in each room that use mains electricity
Living room		
Kitchen		
Bathroom		
Garage		
My bedroom		
Toilet		
Other rooms		

(a) Copy a table like this one into your book. Fill it in with the appliances in your house.

(b) Write a short paragraph to describe what life would be like for you without electricity. Use lots of "Wow!" words.

Aiming higher

2   Spot the five dangers in the picture.

(a) Write a sentence for each saying what is wrong and how it can be avoided.

(b) Explain what danger each safety rule on the opposite page might prevent.

How well am I doing?

On track

I can name at least ten appliances that use electricity.

Aiming higher

I can explain how to prevent danger caused by electricity.

25 What components are used in circuits?

- Electrical circuits are made from components.
- You can draw electrical circuits using these components.

Simple electrical circuits always contain cells or batteries to give the circuit the electricity to work. They might contain lamps (bulbs), electric motors and buzzers which work when the electricity flows around the circuit. To do this they need to be joined together by wires. Switches are used to stop the electricity flowing.

What components can you use?

Each component has a name which you should learn. A battery has two cells joined together and provides more electricity than just one cell.

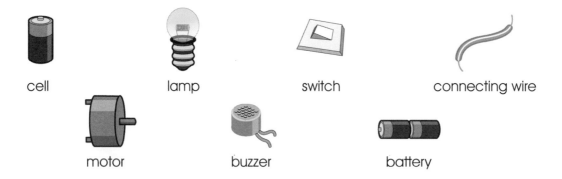

| cell | lamp | switch | connecting wire |

| motor | buzzer | battery |

How can the components be used to make some simple circuits?

These simple circuits help make a bulb light up.

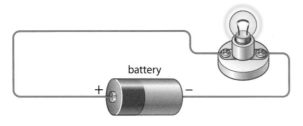

The bulb lights up when these components are joined together.

The switch can be used to turn the circuit on or off.

Component

The basic parts of an electrical circuit.

Electrical circuit

A path for electricity to flow.

On track

1. Ms O'Rourke showed her class this table. It shows drawings of components, their names and what each one does. It has been mixed up.

Component	Name	What does it do?
	Cell	Makes a noise
	Switch	Turns around
	Wires	Lights up
	Motor	Provides electricity
	Buzzer	Turn the circuit on or off
	Lamp	Provides more electricity
	Battery	Joins the components together

   (a) Redraw the table. Draw each component, give it the right name and say what it does.

   (b) Explain the difference between a cell and a battery.

Aiming higher

2. Draw the following circuits using the correct components
   (a) A cell, no switch and a motor.
   (b) A cell, a buzzer, a switch and connecting wires.
   (c) A battery, two bulbs and connecting wires.
   (d) A battery, a motor, a switch and connecting wires.
   (e) A battery, a switch, a bulb, a motor and connecting wires.

How well am I doing?

On track

I can name some of the most common components used in a circuit.

Aiming higher

I can draw a circuit using the correct components.

26 What do you need for an electrical circuit to work?

- **Electrical circuits work when different components are wired up correctly.**

- **Circuits may not work for a variety of reasons.**

Cells are good, safe sources of electricity. Two or more cells connected together make a battery. For a circuit to work, electricity needs to leave one end of the cell, go around the circuit and return to the other end. Circuits can contain components like bulbs and motors that work when electricity flows through them.

How do you make a working circuit?

First of all you need some electricity. The cells in this battery **only work** when the + and – ends of the two cells touch.

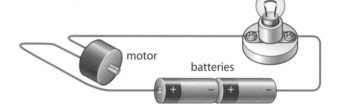

Next you have to make a complete circuit.

You do this by connecting all the components together with wires.

Why do some circuits not work?

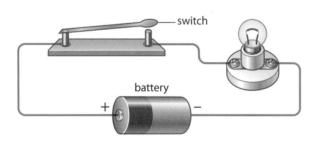

This circuit does not work because the open switch leaves a gap in the circuit. Electricity cannot flow around the circuit.

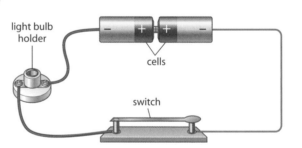

Two things are wrong with this circuit. The cells are not connected correctly and there is no bulb in the bulb holder.

Cell

A device that provides electricity for a circuit to work

Battery

Two or more electrical cells joined together

On track

1   Jessica had a brand new torch.
    It holds two cells joined together as a
    battery. It wasn't working.

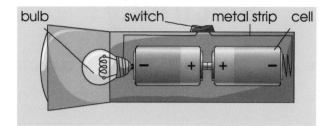

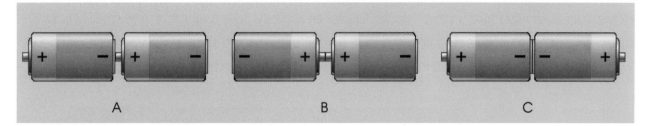

A   B   C

(a) What do the cells do in the torch circuit?

(b) What should Jessica have done to make her torch work?

(c) Which of the arrangements of cells above (A, B and C) will work in
     her torch?

Aiming higher

2   Ms O'Rourke made this circuit. Not all
    the components conduct electricity.

    (a) Write down two reasons why the
         circuit did not work.

    (b) Draw the circuit after it has been
         fixed and made to work.

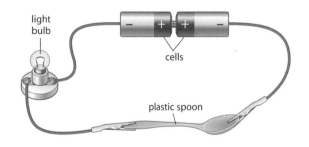

3   Draw a circuit that works with two cells, a bulb and a buzzer.

How well am I doing?

On track

I can say what cells, batteries and
components do in a circuit.

Aiming higher

I can explain what makes a circuit work and
describe what might stop it from working.

27 What kinds of material conduct electricity?

- You can test to find out if a material conducts electricity.
- Some materials let electricity flow through them – others do not.

Have you ever wondered which materials let electricity flow through them and which ones do not? You can test to find this out. If you test enough materials, you can come up with a rule to group materials into electrical **conductors** and electrical **insulators**.

How can you test to find out if a material conducts electricity?

Some materials let electricity flow through them and are called **electrical conductors**. Others don't and are called **electrical insulators**. Tanya and Nathan set up a circuit with two cells, a bulb and some wires. There was a gap in the circuit. The bulb lit up when some materials were put in the gap.

What did they find out?

	Bulb lights up	Bulb stays off
wooden spoon	X	✓
kitchen foil	✓	X
metal fork	✓	X
plastic comb	X	✓
paperclip	✓	X
rubber	X	✓

Here is Tanya's results table.

Tanya said: "The bulb lights up when anything made of metal is put in the gap. It stays off when a non-metal is put in the gap."

She came up with a rule: "Metals are good **electrical conductors** and non-metals are good **electrical insulators**."

Electrical conductor

A material that lets electricity flow through it easily.

Electrical insulator

A material that electricity finds it hard to flow through.

On track

1   Tanya had a closer look at the wires they used in their circuit.

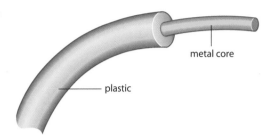

metal core

plastic

She noticed they were made out of two different materials.

(a) Which part of the wire is made out of an electrical conductor?

(b) Explain why the wire is covered with plastic.

(c) How could she test to see if she was right?

Aiming higher

2   Tanya tested some more materials to see if they conducted electricity.

    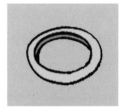

feather   metal key   a ring pull   stone   gold ring

(a) Use their rule to sort the materials into electrical conductors and insulators.

(b) Write down the names of two more materials that are electrical conductors and two that are electrical insulators.

How well am I doing?

On track

I can describe how to test to see if a material conducts electricity.

Aiming higher

I can use a rule to say if a material might conduct electricity or not.

28 How do switches work?

- Many household devices have switches.

- All switches work in basically the same way.

Your TV, lights, washing machine and DVD recorder all have an **on/off switch**. Switches save a lot of electricity by turning the device off when it is not in use. When switches are on, electricity flows around the circuit and the device works. It does not matter where you place the switch in the circuit: it will still work!

Why do devices have on/off switches?

TV	household lights	washing machine
DVD recorder	mobile phone	computer

All of these household devices have a switch that turns the device on and off. This saves a lot of electricity by turning the device off when it is not in use.

How easy is it to make a simple switch?

Look at how these switches have been made out of everyday materials. These switches are only safe to use with batteries.

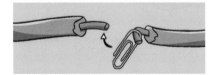

The paperclip acts here as a switch. It links on to one wire. As you see it the switch is open. If the paperclip moves to touch the other wire, the switch closes and electricity flows.

This switch has a springy strip of metal. The picture shows it open. If you press it down onto the drawing pin, the circuit will be completed and electricity will flow through.

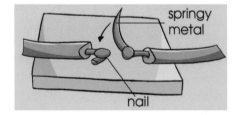

springy metal

nail

cardboard — metal foil

paper fasteners

This switch has wires fixed with paper fasteners onto a piece of card. The other side of the card has some metal foil attached. When the card is pressed together the switch is on.

Switch

A component that makes or breaks a complete circuit.

Device

A useful piece of equipment such as a television or computer.

On track

1 Here are some things you might have in your home.

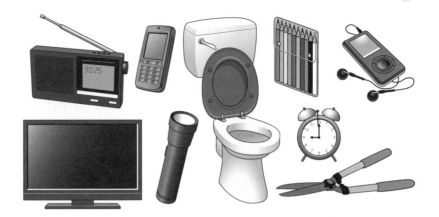

(a) Which of these has an on/off switch?

(b) Give a good reason why it is useful for a device to have an on/off switch.

Aiming higher

2 Look at this circuit. It contains a "paperclip" switch.

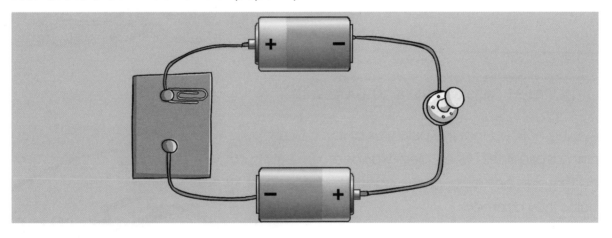

(a) The switch is open. What will happen in the circuit?

(b) What will happen in the circuit when the switch is closed?

(c) Describe in your own words how a switch works.

(d) Could a matchstick be used instead of a paperclip? Explain your answer.

How well am I doing?

On track

I can name five household devices that contain a switch.

Aiming higher

I can explain how a switch works.

29 What makes bulbs brighter or dimmer in a circuit?

- Fair tests help you find out the "brightness rule".
- Adding more cells makes bulbs glow brighter in a circuit.

You can test different circuits to find out how changing the number of bulbs and cells affects the **brightness**. You can come up with a **rule** that helps you predict what might happen in a circuit you have not made yet. That's clever science!

How do you test to find out the "brightness rule"?

Ayesha wanted to find out how she might change the brightness of a bulb.

To make her circuits easy to compare, Ayesha decided to change the number of bulbs and keep everything else the same.

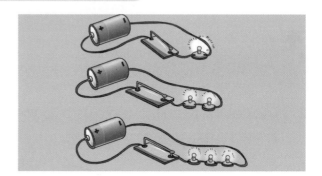

What rules did Ayesha come up with?

Ayesha noticed that the bulb was at its normal brightness when there was one battery and one bulb. As she added more bulbs they dimmed.

She came up with two **rules**.

1   "If the number of bulbs and cells are the same, the brightness will be normal."

2   "The bulbs will be dimmer than normal if there are more bulbs than cells."

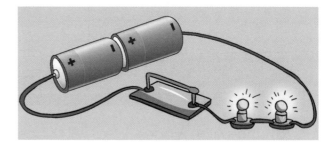

She used her rules to predict that bulbs will light to normal brightness in a circuit with two cells and two bulbs. So she tried it out.

She was right. They were good rules.

Predict

To say what might happen.

Scientific test

A way of doing an experiment so that it is perfectly fair.

On track

1   Ayesha thought more about her test.

	What she kept the same	What she changed	What she observed
number of bulbs			
type of bulb			
number of cells			
brightness of the bulb(s)			

(a) What question did Ayesha test?

(b) Copy out the table and tick the correct boxes.

Aiming higher

2   Ayesha then tested another rule. "The bulbs will be brighter than normal if there are more batteries than bulbs."

	What she kept the same	What she changed	What she observed
number of bulbs			
type of bulb			
number of cells			
brightness of the bulb(s)			

(a) Copy the table. Tick the correct boxes to make Ayesha's second test fair.

(b) Draw the circuits she might have made.

(c) Label them to show the names of the parts.

How well am I doing?

On track

I can design a fair test.

Aiming higher

I can use the "brightness rules" correctly to make predictions and test them out.

Index